FIRST, I TURN OFF THE LIGHT

Katy Mack's poems have appeared widely in publications including *The Poetry Review, Ambit, Poem International, Poetry Birmingham Literary Journal,* and *Perverse*. She has also been commended in The Troubadour International Poetry Prize. She completed her creative writing PhD in poetry at UEA in 2022 and is currently a Research Impact Fellow at The University of Sussex.

CONTENTS

WHAT I HAVEN'T SAID IS   9

WHEN THE SCARECROWS COME, YOU MUST NOT QUESTION WHY   10

WHEN IT CAME   11

THE CLOWN UPSTAIRS   12

A MIX UP   13

WHEN IT COMES AS A HERON   15

SCREEN SAVER   16

WHAT THE WATER DOES   17

AND SO, I STARTED TO DRESS UP AS A SHARK   19

MY BIG NIGHT OUT   21

WHERE THE THOUGHTS GO   22

BED   24

NOW WE ARE NOT HAVING A BABY   25

THE WOMAN IN THE MIRROR   26

WHAT HAPPENS DURING THE BREATHING EXERCISE   28

A DAY IN THE CLUB OF PERPETUAL HAPPINESS   30

IN THE PLAY I SAW ABOUT A DOOR-TO-DOOR   31

HOOVER SALESMAN   31

SOME NIGHTS   32

EMILY, IN MANY THINGS: A SEQUENCE

EMILY, IN MANY THINGS   35

INVENTORY OF THE CONTENTS OF EMILY'S POCKET   36

WHAT WAS SHE?   38

EMILY'S WAFERS   39

CHARLOTTE'S ALTERATIONS (I)   40

CHARLOTTE'S ALTERATIONS (II)   41

EMILY IS UNWELL   42

NOTES   45

ACKNOWLEDGEMENTS   47

ISBN: 978-1-916938-21-2

Cover designed by Aaron Kent

Edited and Typeset by Aaron Kent

Broken Sleep Books Ltd
PO BOX 102
Llandysul
SA44 9BG

First, I Turn Off the Light

Katy Mack

Broken Sleep Books

Obsessive-Compulsive Disorder (OCD) is a common, chronic, and long-lasting disorder in which a person has uncontrollable, reoccurring thoughts (obsessions) and/or behaviors (compulsions) that he or she feels the urge to repeat over and over.
— Definition from The National Institute of Mental Health

We are all haunted houses.
— H. D.

WHAT I HAVEN'T SAID IS

When I heard about the woman who ate her bedroom wall –
each day a new piece of plaster, chipped off
and choked down with a cup of warm water –
my mouth went dry, a taste of chalk and earth.
I too keep rocks in my stomach, small and quiet,
though I've never told you.
Just as I've never mentioned the tapping
from inside the skirting board,
or the light switch that fizzes in the dark,
sometimes the pine trees on the wallpaper
nod from side to side
and I can't tell if it's a warning
or an invitation.
But I do know that each time
I don't say this I grow heavier
and the walls which keep us safe
are getting thin.

WHEN THE SCARECROWS COME, YOU MUST NOT QUESTION WHY

Instead, let them in like old friends,
allow them to hang their ragamuffin coats
and sit at your table on the steadiest chairs.
Let them eat the decent bread
and drink the cider you've been saving.
They may talk amongst themselves in the low hum
of telegraph wires on a hot summer's day,
they may swoop their pumpkin heads,
or unfasten their patchwork smiles,
but you mustn't read too much into it.
Affect an air of absolute self-assurance:
wear a casual blazer, unscrew the jar of pickled onions
like someone who owns many jars of pickled onions.
If one of them looks at you directly, look back
but not too intently; it has been said
that staring into the eyes of a scarecrow
is like peering down the shafts of great wells –
some have been known to slip.
Of course, not everyone knows the way of scarecrows;
some can hear the click of the garden gate
free from the feeling that something inside
is unlatching. Imagine being such a person –
arranging tumblers along a kitchen shelf,
taking the small, clean weight of a whole glass in your hand,
turning each one against the light and simply thinking
yes, this glass is empty, and yes, this one, empty also,
like someone who really believes it.

WHEN IT CAME

I thought it would announce itself
with a knock on the door
at an unfamiliar hour.
Or else rush in on a sudden gust
forcing the crack in our bedroom window,
the curtains blown apart.
In fact, there was no shattered glass
on the carpet, no telephone receiver dangling.
I hardly even noticed
the sun's pulse had quickened
against the kitchen floorboards,
a taste of rain clinging
to the backs of our throats,
lodged like a wishbone.

THE CLOWN UPSTAIRS

His pointed feet walk the tightrope of the brick wall
behind me as I head back from the corner shop.
He holds plastic tulips in one hand,
a Costcutter bag swinging from the other.
I turn around, suddenly, and catch his painted grin
peeking out from behind a tree – *here I am!*

When I'm chopping onions
in the kitchen, I hear him clinking bottles upstairs
and fancy that he's hosting a party –
other clowns arriving (some happy, some sad),
all of them squeezing into his one bedroom flat,
dogs in velvet ruffs whining from the windows,
the sound of tiny accordions ringing in my ears.
Sometimes he leaves gifts on my doormat:
sugared cigarettes, and a small red fish
which rocks from side to side in my palm
indicating that I, too, am out of kilter.

But the clown upstairs is often in good spirits,
his laugh enters my bedroom,
bouncing off the four walls
like a face in a hall of mirrors.
Other nights he is so quiet I begin to think
he has gone away entirely,
until the morning
when the soured lemonade of his breath
crouches in the corridor
and I'm mistaken.

A MIX UP

They had gotten the time of the wedding
and the time of the funeral mixed up.
'Such a shame', a guest commented to his wife,
as it was the perfect day for it –
the sun glinting against a wide, unending sea
and the congregation crammed into the aisles,
their pockets filled with dried petals,
the sense of anticipation palpable
as the long, silent car drew up outside.
An hour later, she crossed the threshold into the church
her white gown billowing,
her hair strewn with roses,
as the footsteps rang out on the flagstones
to rows of men in black coats,
their tall hats like chimney pots,
the groom was nowhere to be seen.
'Isn't it curious,' the gentlemen observed outside
after the proceedings had taken place
'how there is a strange kind of symmetry to everything.'
Everyone nodded in agreement, the thin smoke
from their elongated cigarettes offering itself up
to the mist and drizzle. While behind them,
the bride started her solemn procession
down the uneven steps to the sea,
which, many noted, had been such a source of comfort
throughout the day – its symbolism of renewal
and regeneration so fitting.
Others reflected quietly to themselves

that the sea left them with a sensation of weariness,
something to do with its constant raging
against the shoreline, only to break
and be pulled, inevitably, back again.

WHEN IT COMES AS A HERON

If I turn my back
shadows collect
along the tall fold of the curtain,
the umbrella's neck arches.
The carving fork,
secure in the drawer
where I left it, will develop
a single, grasping talon;
the slender mouths of scissors
turn and open.
I'll be in the shower,
with my mind somewhere else,
and feel its presence,
hot breath edging, slowly,
up the length of my spine
until nothing inside me flinches,
the way the lake doesn't flinch –
all its darting things
just freeze
in the split second
before the snap.

SCREEN SAVER

Facedown onto the kitchen tiles
I pick it up turn it over not realising
the damage until the backlight reveals
a cracked rectangle of sun over
a new image: the park only not the park
I remember – here the lamp posts jut
at impossible angles like fractured bones
parents are queuing in crooked lines
for the ice-cream van – their kids
hanging in the playground lopsided
on the monkey bars and you sitting
on the bench with your smile split
in two waiting for our daughter who is
midway down the helter-skelter
her small laugh caught in that metal tunnel
at the point before she might hurtle out
headfirst into a puddle of murky water
though when I look again
it's not really a puddle
not really water
but splintered glass
resting on the palm of my hand.

WHAT THE WATER DOES

It starts as a noise
from the bathroom – *drip, drip, drip,*
but when I check
the room is dry as a bone.
The next night it happens again,
and every night thereafter.
Each time I expect to catch
the bath's full belly, quivering
in the dark. I lie very still
unable to shake the thought of water,
contorting itself through pipes
underneath floorboards –
a boa constrictor
easing its way into my room,
taking the shape of everything it touches.
I seal all the cracks in the house
with wire wool and cloth
and, for a while, the dripping subsides
until I'm on my way to work or in a coffee shop
and the noise will start again,
only louder this time, more insistent.
Soon, water creeps up through the concrete,
puddles swell into streams
and it isn't long before
the whole length of street is writhing,
birds gliding along the surface.
A dark ring appears
at the bottom of my jeans –

sliding upwards,
my pockets growing heavy
until I feel it enter
making its way into
the pit of my stomach,
where it starts expanding.

AND SO, I STARTED TO DRESS UP AS A SHARK

I enjoy my newfound height –
how people hold doors open as I approach them,
and strangers stop me in the street for selfies
asking if they may rest their heads
upon my white, pillowy underbelly.
I wear the suit so often that friends and loved ones
forget I'm in there
and address their comments to the arrow-shaped head
looming just above my own,
making jokes about custard
while jabbing their pink elbows into my side.
I sleep often – deep, thick dreams
in which I'm lying in a field of grass, blades turning
in the breeze, stripes of sunlight over my arms and legs,
while in the undergrowth,
shadows flash, start to circle in.
When I Google sharks, I learn
that they lack the capacity to dream and so
I empty my head of difficult thoughts,
drip by drip. But I keep coming back
to that house party a few weeks ago,
where a girl cut her hand on some glass
the blood trickling down her arm,
and how in the slim moments before the panic,
frenzy tingled up my spine.
How my mouth went dry,
my skin tightened like leather
and in the mirror, for a second,

I caught myself –
a pair of eyes looking out
from the darkness between
row upon row of jagged teeth.

MY BIG NIGHT OUT

You've gone away for the weekend   so I'm going to drag myself
out for the night   get pig-drunk at the bar   steal the fattest chip
from   my own plate   when my back is turned. I'll run into the
road with a traffic cone on my head   darting past cars in the rain
ketchup stained like a nosebleed down the front of my new white
t-shirt   and myself in pursuit   out of breath in wet socks. On
the walk home I'll puke behind a tree   while holding my hair back
and because you're not there   I'll promise myself   *it's ok, it's all
going to be ok*   but the next morning I'm already plucking at the
frayed edges of every bad thing I've ever done while I make coffee
stuff a pillow into a fresh cover forcing it in because you'll be back
soon   and if you're not   I'm not sure what I'll do with myself.

WHERE THE THOUGHTS GO

I think of my heart
as a pocket watch
all those tiny components
ticking, neatly, inside my chest,
which I have come to regard
as a bureau of polished oak
drawers filled with air,
inside the body,
which I think of
as a grand house
closed up for the winter,
all its curtains drawn,
floorboards creaking
from inside the head
which I have come to regard
as a room in the attic –
its dust swept beneath a bed,
an empty rocking-chair
by the fireplace,
which I am learning
to think of as the mind –
relieved of its kindling.
I have come to regard
the difficult thoughts
as outsiders, fox-like, they hiss
and rustle about the woodshed,
I ignore their crunching
up and down the gravel path,

or the noise
from the front door
as it pounds
and it pounds
and it pounds.

BED

If I lie here and do not move
then the days will wash over me.
I eat only clear soup
and can't stomach the thought of crumbs,
wriggling in the bed like ants.
Soon, the grey outline of a woman's body
forms on the taut linen,
a head's vague shape worn
across the headboard
and somewhere buried inside the pillow –
a heartbeat, faint but persistent,
edging me back to the sound of next door's radio.
Your voice from the doorway
saying 'she's up' while handing me bread and milk,
as I lie underneath the muddled piles of blankets
which are heavy as rainfall
and all the while water is lapping, steadily,
up the bed frame.

NOW WE ARE NOT HAVING A BABY

tiny babies are bobbing
in my glass of sparkling water,
their bodies dissolving between my fingertips
as I try to pluck one out and hold it to the light.
Babies of all different sizes crawling along the carpet,
the smaller ones climbing into my worn-out trainers
where they sleep all day
and scream into the night. If I want to leave
I must empty each shoe gently,
like someone removing a scorpion.
Some of the larger babies are propped up
along the kitchen shelf, nestling
amongst the bottles of gin and bags of self-raising flour,
a chubby hand emerges from the rubbish bin,
the inner part of a discarded onion glistening in its palm,
as if it were holding up a small, translucent heart
and asking: 'surely, you didn't mean to throw this away
did you?' I kiss each one goodbye, in turn,
and swear I'll be back before they know it.
They peer from the window
as I vanish behind a corner,
their faces starting to quiver
the way a house might
in the seconds before it collapses.

THE WOMAN IN THE MIRROR

I was as astonished as anyone to find the woman on the other side
of the convex mirror, her face so like my own
only aged in the antique glass. At first, I found her disregard
for my usual routines refreshing: fresh sheets and polished brass,
the apples cut into segments, the nightly urge to light a candle.
She didn't need to plump up her life like an over-stuffed cushion,
instead, she sat in her easy chair letting the days pass through
the house like a breeze from an open window.
But soon things changed. I arranged the spring flowers in a tall vase
only to see the same vase in the mirror with nothing inside it –
save a pool of musty water and a grey, clinging stench.
Friends would come over for dinner and we would drink cold beers
and talk, while the woman in the mirror laughed, animatedly,
to a room with no one in it. One evening, when I was brushing
my teeth, as normal, I caught her pressing her mouth against the glass
and pulling out a large yellow tooth, tossing it in the sink
into a pile of other loose teeth, shining like spare pennies.
After that I couldn't bear the sight of her –
the broad, empty smile spreading over her face.
I wanted to wipe her away, as you might a dirty mark,
or, in more exasperated moments, I even considered taking a hammer
and smashing the glass across the rug.
Instead, I got rid of the mirror, placing it outside
with the old clothes and broken furniture
hoping a passerby would take it far away.
All that remained was a faded, gaping circle on the wallpaper
which is still there, although I'm a much older woman
and it's been many years since I've seen the woman in the mirror,

I wonder if she'd even recognise me now,
what she'd make of what I've become
of my life and of the terrible mess I've made,
and keep making, of it all.

WHAT HAPPENS DURING THE BREATHING EXERCISE

Try to imagine you're climbing up a tall mountain
    the woman tells me in a soft voice,

and my mind turns to those two men
    in that documentary we saw,

only this time we're the ones traversing the icy edifice
    in sturdy boots, with only a length of rope

connecting us. So precariously balanced
    up there, passing our body mass

back and forth like small bags of sugar –
    me with an ice axe

searching out a foothold in the crevices,
    and you below on the thin shelf

steadying the line as it bucks and sways.
    I'm trying not to look down

to the miles of faceless snow beneath,
    focusing, instead, on the summit

and she asks that I imagine climbing over its verge,
    the lightness of the specific kind of air

at the top. I'm told to let out a heavy exhale –
    all that rubble I've been carrying

deep in my chest. Only, I can't stop thinking
    of the two men in that documentary,

of what happened to them in the final moments
    and I'm suddenly conscious

of the weight of my breath
    as it escapes from the room I'm sitting in

and tumbles back down that length of rope
    into your open mouth,

filling up your lungs with hail.

A DAY IN THE CLUB OF PERPETUAL HAPPINESS

The members of the club are all exceedingly happy. Many are married. Some with children, some with minute pet dogs – their brilliant white fur clipped in neat balls about the ankles, as if they had just padded through over-whipped cream. Others are single, but this does not impede their overall happiness – there's no drifting through empty corridors or sitting alone at the dinner table. In fact, everyone in the club gets on perfectly and every morning there is a baking competition in the windowless basement, where members make eclairs double dipped in dark chocolate. The chief pâtissier does his rounds, taking bites from each delectable treat. He declares this one of his top ten happiest moments, smacking his lips for emphasis. No one is crowned baking champion as it was decreed that each member was already a winner in his or her own distinctive, and equally exceptional, way. In the afternoon, there is a guided group mediation taken outside in the walled yard; every participant is invited to picture their own individual happiness as taking the form of a large, billowing cloud, which must be pulled down from the heavens (for, everyone knows, happiness is a fleeting thing) and sliced into twenty even portions, shared amongst the group. In the evening, members attend the daily feast of happiness with its tables of warm succulent meats and its balls of ice cream, melting. After dinner, the fat, gold moon makes a special appearance and each person thanks him, in turn, for his gift of happiness. When the revelries are completed, the staff throw away the fallen soufflé and greyhounds gnaw at the carcasses, prizing off the precious meat. Upstairs the members are tucked up in their beds, settling into a night of contented and uninterrupted sleep, while above them stars flit and the wild, inconstant sky goes about its usual business.

IN THE PLAY I SAW ABOUT A DOOR-TO-DOOR HOOVER SALESMAN

Perhaps it was because his teeth were too straight,
or the way his glasses changed from dark to transparent
depending on the slant of the spotlight,
or that, at certain angles, you could see the faint 'O'
of a nipple through his short-sleeved shirt –
but somehow, we knew this was not a man to be trusted.
He had a secret alright, unsightly, like a ferret up a trouser leg.
It didn't matter about his stable home life,
his wife, three plump children at the flat above the arcade.
Secrets like that were dirty then,
sticky, push them right to the back of the sofa,
but still there's a black ridge left beneath a fingernail.
His secret was no different, only
it happened to be my secret too.
When the big reveal came they hauled it out of him
kicking and screaming – *slap*! – onto the stage,
the auditorium fell silent;
my secret turned and scurried back
into my open mouth
burrowing itself into my chest.
Nothing would prize it out,
not a lullaby or a scrap of raw meat.
Once I thought of feeding the entire arm of a hoover
down there like a bad party trick:
each coil snaking down my windpipe,
my lungs vibrating like a tin can.
Even now, after I've told you all of this,
I'm still here dragging the nozzle
over the white living room carpet
on my hands and knees.

SOME NIGHTS

Some nights we are so magnificent, you and I, we could loosen the stars
from their constellations and flick them aside like dead flies.

Other nights we are pin-prick small and folded away under the bed
like we are playing sleeping lions and will be disqualified for breathing.

Some nights I feel the pulse of your sleep as your limbs twist round
dancing a slow dance and won't risk waking in case the music stops.

Other nights we have a glass of milk and half a valium
and wonder why we find numbness preferable to living.

Some nights you place your hand on my spine and count each vertebra
like gold coins, like you know the cost of things and I am terribly dear.

Some nights we are not like anything at all, you and I,
and I cannot comprehend that it's not enough.

Emily, in many things: a sequence

EMILY, IN MANY THINGS

They say she's on the other side
of the door to the sealed room,
in the creak
of the china-stacked dresser,
the scrape of the chair's leg
along the flagstones.

She's in the shift
of the bone-dry sticks
in the swept hearth,
the subdued tick
deep in the tall clock's
hollow chest.

She's in the resistance
of the iron-forged bolt,
and the click
of the door's latch
as it lifts
and lifts, once again.

INVENTORY OF THE CONTENTS OF EMILY'S POCKET

An apple core   a bone-handled comb
with five teeth missing   a candle stub
a dandelion's head   half-blown out.

An envelope, sealed, with nothing inside.

Dried fish scales sewn onto satin
in the shape of forget-me-nots.

A neatly clipped blade of grass   a sprig of heather.
The hook-and-eye fastener of a Sunday dress.

Black ink   jet   keys   a quarter yard of lace.

A looking glass with no glass.

A Venetian mask   Keeper's brown leather muzzle
nibs a bottle of opium
to bring back *wildering* thoughts.

A pocket watch stopped at 2 o'clock, exactly.
Pressed flowers. A goose-quill. Ripped parchment.

Sewing box with the words *here I am* etched inside.
Thread   thimbles torn-up fabric. A folded umbrella.

The trapped vapour of solid things
such as whin yellow gorse peat.

A small ring set with a zircon stone –

the mineral commonly mistaken for diamonds
owing to its flitting, concealed light.

WHAT WAS SHE?

'Her tendency to seclusion'
'Solitude-loving raven'
'She rarely crossed the threshold–'
'One who is your other self'
'Long strides over rough earth'
'Her lips compressed into stone'
'Making haste to leave us'.

EMILY'S WAFERS

U no secrets I

(Bear) it in mind

UR all price

Faithful + firm

Always at home

I can't get out

CHARLOTTE'S ALTERATIONS (I)

THOU *for* thou
wanderer *for* Wanderer
weep *for* yearn
mother *for* Mother
house *for* House
safe *for* ________

CHARLOTTE'S ALTERATIONS (II)

thou *becomes thou*
laid at rest *becomes* resting
winter *becomes* frozen
alone— *becomes* alone.

EMILY IS UNWELL

Illness hangs over this house like a heavy, scheming cloud.
Father puts another black cross in his pocketbook.
We've stoked each fire, lined every curtain,
put on our winter furs.

Still Emily's lips are turning purple. Her skin,
once as translucent as tracing paper, now ivory.
Ladies from the village make their daily visit.
Precious girl, they shriek, like magpies clustered at her feet.

They adorn her with ribbons, apply rouge to her cheeks.
Braiding the tight fist of her knotted hair, until she's pretty
as a picture. We wash her body, wrap her in the finest silk,
so she gleams for the Vicar who comes twice a day.

He bids us unburden our souls on the bedroom floor,
our inky hearts peeled till there's nothing left.
Sister, oh dear sister, whatever would I do without you?
Still she lies there, quiet as a bone-handled knife.

The Physician bleeds her daily now, but her rigid veins
won't open up. Curious, unyielding creature.
She is lost to us. Father says, shutting his pocketbook.
Little does he know; it is we who are lost.

'Inventory of the contents of Emily's pocket' - Some of these images are taken from objects the Brontës were said to have had in their possession, as well as items found at the Brontë Parsonage Museum in Haworth. Included among these images is, notably, the bone-handled comb Emily used on the morning of her death, when, weakened by illness, she attempted to brush her hair only to drop the comb into the fire. Her servant, Martha Brown, entered the room and pulled the comb out however five of its teeth had already been singed in the flames. There is also mention of the sewing box of painted wood which held clothing fasteners, ribbons and fragments of broken jewellery. Found inside the box was a pair of linked jet ovals with Charlotte and Emily's names scratched inside.

'What was she?' - Beyond her poems and the drafts of her novel very little archival material remains of Emily Brontë's writing or correspondence with others. This poem uses extracts of phrases and observations taken from those around Emily. They include: a series of conversational phrases taken from Charlotte Brontë's memories of her sister; W. S. Williams's recollections of Emily which he recounted in a letter to Charlotte after Emily's death; and Mrs Gaskell's retelling of a scene where Emily beats her disobedient dog, Keeper, after he was found sleeping on a forbidden bed in the Parsonage, Emily's home throughout her life.

'Emily's wafers' - These phrases are taken from a white packet of 'Clarke's Enigmatic Puzzle Wafers' found in Emily's desk and paint box. Such wafers were used to seal correspondences and were intended, in part, to ensure that the contents of the envelope were not tampered with. They also became another method of correspondence between the sender and the recipient of the letter, in some cases a form of private joke or dialogue between the two.

'Charlotte's alterations (i)' and 'Charlotte's alterations (ii)' - In the autumn of 1845 Charlotte famously lighted upon Emily's poems 'accidentally' while searching through her sister's belongings — this invasion of privacy was infuriating to Emily. In the years following Emily's death, Charlotte went back through Emily's poems and made a series of editorial alterations. In some cases, these edits were small modifications to words and syntax, in others, Charlotte rewrote whole stanzas. These changes mainly appear in Emily's poems 'The Night-Wind', 'The First Blue-Stocking' and 'No Coward Soul is Mine'.

ACKNOWLEDGEMENTS

Thanks are due to the following publications in which some of these poems first appeared. 'When the scarecrows come, you must not question why' in *Poetry Review* 112, 2022; 'And so, I started to dress up as a shark' in *Perverse* 7A; 'In the play I saw about the door-to-door Hoover salesman' in *Poetry Birmingham Literary Journal* 5, 2020; 'Some nights' in *Ambit* 222, 2015.

I am grateful to those who have generously taken the time to read, edit, and encourage the writing of these poems. Special thanks are due to Denise Riley, Jon Cook, Rebecca Goss, Mary Powell, and Roxy Dunn, and to the members of the NT writing workshop.

Finally, my love and thanks to my family and friends for their support over the years. And with special thanks to my partner, Lea.

LAY OUT YOUR UNREST